Taurus

Also by Sally Kirkman

Aries
Gemini
Cancer
Leo
Virgo
Libra
Scorpio
Sagittarius
Capricorn
Aquarius
Pisces

SALLY KIRKMAN

Taurus

The Art of Living Well and Finding
Happiness According to Your Star Sign

HODDER

First published in Great Britain in 2018 by Hodder & Stoughton
An Hachette UK company

8

Copyright © Sally Kirkman 2018

A CIP catalogue record for this title is available from the British Library

Hardback ISBN 978 1 473 67669 5

Typeset in Celeste 11.5/17 pt by Palimpsest Book Production Limited,
Falkirk, Stirlingshire

Printed in the United States of America by LSC Communications

Hodder & Stoughton policy is to use papers that are natural,
renewable and recyclable products and made from wood grown in
sustainable forests. The logging and manufacturing processes are expected
to conform to the environmental regulations of the country of origin.

Hodder & Stoughton Ltd
Carmelite House
50 Victoria Embankment
London EC4Y 0DZ

www.hodder.co.uk

Contents

· · · · ·

Introduction

• • • • •

Before computers, books or a shared language, people were fascinated by the movement of the stars and planets. They created stories and myths around them. We know that the Babylonians were one of the first people to record the zodiac, a few hundred years BC.

In ancient times, people experienced a close connection to the earth and the celestial realm. The adage 'As above, so below', that the movement of the planets and stars mirrored life on earth and human affairs, made perfect sense. Essentially, we were all one, and ancient people sought symbolic meaning in everything around them.

We are living in a very different world now, in

which scientific truth is paramount; yet many people are still seeking meaning. In a world where you have an abundance of choice, dominated by the social media culture that allows complete visibility into other people's lives, it can be hard to feel you belong or find purpose or think that the choices you are making are the right ones.

It's this calling for something more, the sense that there's a more profound truth beyond the objective and scientific, that leads people to astrology and similar disciplines that embrace a universal truth, an intuitive knowingness. Today astrology has a lot in common with spirituality, meditation, the Law of Attraction, a desire to know the cosmic order of things.

Astrology means 'language of the stars' and people today are rediscovering the usefulness of ancient wisdom. The universe is always talking to you; there are signs if you listen and the more you tune in, the more you feel guided by life. This is one of astrology's significant benefits, helping you to make sense of an increasingly unpredictable world.

Used well, astrology can guide you in making the best possible decisions in your life. It's an essential skill in your personal toolbox that enables you to navigate the ups and downs of life consciously and efficiently.

About this book

Astrology is an ancient art that helps you find meaning in the world. The majority of people to this day know their star sign, and horoscopes are growing increasingly popular in the media and online.

The modern reader understands that star signs are a helpful reference point in life. They not only offer valuable self-insight and guidance, but are indispensable when it comes to understanding other people, and living and working together in harmony.

This new and innovative pocket guide updates the ancient tradition of astrology to make it relevant and topical for today. It distils the wisdom of the star signs into an up-to-date format that's easy to read and digest, and fun and informative too. Covering a broad range of topics, it offers you insight and understanding into many different areas of your life. There are some unique sections you won't find anywhere else.

The style of the guide is geared towards you being able to maximise your strengths, so you can live well and use your knowledge of your star sign to your advantage. The more in tune you are with your zodiac sign, the higher your potential to lead a happy and fulfilled life.

The guide starts with a quick introduction to your star sign, in bullet point format. This not only reveals your star sign's ancient ruling principles, but brings astrology up-to-date, with your star sign mission, an appropriate quote for your sign and how best to describe your star sign in a tweet.

The first chapter is called 'Be True To Your Sign' and is one of the most important sections in the guide. It's a comprehensive look at all aspects of your star sign, helping define what makes you special, and explaining how the rich symbolism of your zodiac sign can reveal more about your character. For example, being born at a specific time of year and in a particular season is significant in itself.

This chapter focuses in depth on the individual attributes of your star sign in a way that's positive and uplifting. It offers a holistic view of your sign and is meant to inspire you. Within this section, you find out the reasons why your star sign traits and characteristics are unique to you.

There's a separate chapter towards the end of the guide that takes this star sign information to a new level. It's called 'Your Cosmic Gifts and Talents' and tells you what's individual about you from your star sign perspective. Most importantly, it highlights your skills and strengths, offering you clear examples of how to make the most of your natural birthright.

The guide touches on another important aspect of your star sign, in the chapters entitled 'Your Shadow Side' and 'Your Star Sign Secrets'. This reveals the potential weaknesses inherent within your star sign, and the tricks and habits you can fall into if you're not aware of them. The star sign secrets might surprise you.

There's guidance here about what you can focus on to minimise the shadow side of your star sign, and this is linked in particular to your opposite sign of the zodiac. You learn how opposing forces complement each other when you hold both ends of the spectrum, enabling them to work together.

Essentially, the art of astrology is about how to find balance in your life, to gain a sense of universal or cosmic order, so you feel in flow rather than pulled in different directions.

Other chapters in the guide provide revealing information about your love life and sex life. There are cosmic tips on how to work to your star sign strengths so you can attract and keep a fulfilling relationship, and lead a joyful sex life. There's also a guide to your love compatibility with all twelve star signs.

Career, money and prosperity is another essential section in the guide. These chapters offer you vital information on your purpose in life, and how to make the most of your potential out in the world. Your star sign skills and strengths are revealed, including what sort of job or profession suits you.

There are also helpful suggestions about what to avoid and what's not a good choice for you. There's a list of traditional careers associated with your star sign, to give you ideas about where you can excel in life if you require guidance on your future direction.

Also, there are chapters in the book on practical matters, like your health and well-being, your food and diet. These recommend the right kind of exercise for you, and how you can increase your vitality and nurture your mind, body and soul, depending on your star sign. There are individual yoga poses and tarot cards that have been carefully selected for you.

Further chapters reveal unique star sign information about your image and style. This includes whether there's a particular fashion that suits you, and how you can accentuate your look and make the most of your body.

There are even chapters that can help you decide where to go on holiday and who with, and how to decorate your home. There are some fun sections, including ideal gifts for your star sign, and ideas for films, books and music specific to your star sign.

Also, the guide has a comprehensive birthday section so you can find out which famous people share your birthday. You can discover who else is born under your star sign, people who may be your role models and whose careers or gifts you can aspire to. There are celebrity examples throughout the guide too, revealing more about the unique characteristics of your star sign.

At the end of the guide, there's a Question and Answer section, which explains the astrological terms used in the guide. It also offers answers to some general questions that often arise around astrology.

This theme is continued in a useful section entitled Additional Information. This describes the symmetry of astrology and shows you how different patterns connect the twelve star signs. If you're a beginner to astrology, this is your next stage, learning about the elements, the modes and the houses.

View this book as your blueprint, your guide to you and your future destiny. Enjoy discovering astrological revelations about you, and use this pocket guide to learn how to live well and find happiness according to your star sign.

A QUICK GUIDE TO TAURUS

• • • • •

Birthdays: 20 April to 20 May

Zodiac Symbol: The Bull

Ruling Planet: Venus

Mode/Element: Fixed Earth

Colour: Green, colours of the earth

Part of the Body: Neck and throat

Day of the Week: Friday

Top Traits: Reliable, Sensual, Persistent

Your Star Sign Mission: to build solid foundations that are lasting, to savour life fully

Best At: patience, dependability, pleasurable activities, practical common sense, artistic talents, loving nature, nurturing others, making money, enjoying food, creating solid foundations

Weaknesses: stubborn, possessive, coarse, lewd, slides into inertia

Key Phrase: I produce

Taurus Quote: 'Anyone can become a millionaire but to become a billionaire you need an astrologer.' J. P. Morgan

How to describe Taurus in a Tweet: Love, money, pleasure; the master and mistress of self-indulgence. Funny but coarse, persistent but stubborn. No one can budge you

• • • • •

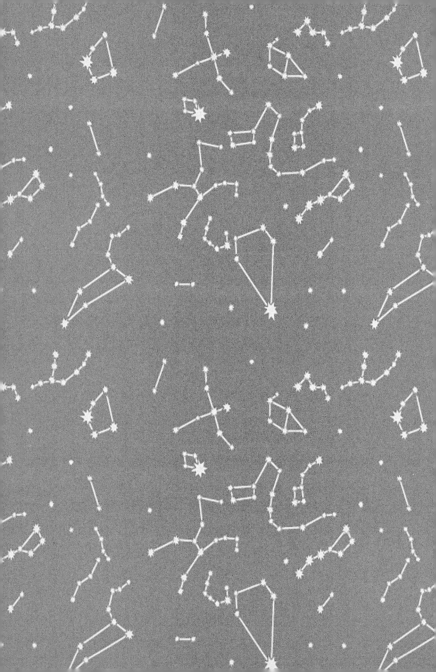

Be True To Your Sign

• • • • •

The Taurus nature leans towards pleasure, and you want to taste, savour, feel, hear and smell the gorgeousness of life in all its glory.

The time when the Sun is in your sign of Taurus, in spring, coincides with one of the most fertile and abundant times of the year. You are one of the earth signs and nature is your playground. If you're a typical Taurus, you'll feel at home with nature and all that it represents: growth, life and fecundity.

In the northern hemisphere, late April and the month of May are synonymous with abundance, a time to make the most of nature's bounty and to tend to your garden.

Maypole dancing takes place during Taurus season, and morris dancers wave their hankies and wiggle their bells. Both traditional events remain symbols of fertility and the blossoming of spring. Taurus season is a time when the lushness of nature overflows and colourful flowers burst into bloom.

Being a Taurus, you are ruled by lovely Venus, representing all the good things in life. Combine this with your earthy nature, and you are the most sensual sign of the zodiac, naturally drawn towards indulgence and the richness of life. If you're a classic Taurus, you have a healthy appreciation for simple pleasures.

The element of earth is slow-moving, and after the first rush of spring, it's time to take stock. Earth signs want to know what they can produce and create in life and your sign, in particular, is the builder and artist of the zodiac.

You're not usually interested in starting over but instead like working with what's available and making the most of what you've got. Your skill comes from fashioning something new from what is readily available.

You don't like to see things go to waste either; instead, you're eager to produce something valuable and long-lasting from what's already emerged. You're the zodiac's grower, someone who wants to bring objects/projects/seeds to fruition and completion.

Your sign is associated with the second house, ruling money and possessions but also other things that are of value. This is a fundamental component of the Taurus character, and you often have a keen appreciation of the things and people in your life that you love.

If you're a typical Taurus, you like to acquire things. You can be something of a collector, whether you're purchasing beautiful objects or something as an investment for the future. As a gardener, you know that tending what you own carefully and attentively is a sound strategy, because it will yield fruit in the future.

You rarely go into something for a short-term fix. Instead, you focus on things of long-term value and often what gives you the most pleasure. An archetypal Taurus is in it for the long haul.

You are one of the most laid-back signs of the zodiac. You have heaps of patience and you rarely rush through life. Instead, you do whatever you can to savour experiences and to make life easy for yourself and others.

You also have a talent for being able to focus on what's relevant and deal with essentials. You are one of the most practical signs of the zodiac and your 'get real', practical common sense means that you don't waste energy. You rarely go off on a tangent; you usually take the simplest and most sensible route to your destination.

These important characteristics mean that even

though you make progress slowly, you never give up, and if any star sign of the zodiac can be said to have staying power, it's you. Your tenacious nature means you get there in the end and you'd aim for quality over quantity any time.

Similarly, when it comes to movement, it's not necessarily something that's high up on the Taurus list of priorities. In fact, being one of the fixed signs, you like to stay put, and you can be very resistant to change.

This has both strengths and weaknesses. It means that you can be incredibly stubborn and refuse to give up on a goal, which is great. It also means that you can be so stubborn that no one can budge you and you miss out. You have to be careful that you don't slow down so much in life that you get a reputation for being boring or immovable.

Being slow to respond means that you're not overly troubled by other people's interference or the more emotional side of life. You get on with it instead. However, just like your zodiac symbol the Bull, who can look incredibly calm and stoic, it's a different matter altogether when you lose it.

The Taurus temper can be ferocious. This is when your formidable strength and power come to the fore and, like the proverbial 'bull in a china shop', you can be uncontrollable and potentially destructive. When you stand your ground and refuse to budge, you're an immovable force.

Outbursts tend to be rare in Taurus' world and thanks to your ruler Venus, you're drawn more towards harmony. It is important to find the right balance between these two.

A typical Taurus has a hearty laugh and a great sense of humour that helps you appreciate whatever life throws your way. Your earthy qualities often extend to swearing and crude behaviour, and you see nothing wrong with that. You're a down-to-earth, hands-on individual and once you know what you want out of life and how to get it, you're on your way. You respect emotional and financial security, and once you're happy with your set-up in life, you can become content and pleased with your lot.

Your Shadow Side

Being a Taurus means that you will go through stages in your lifetime when you rank your level of importance or status according to what you possess in your world. For some, this is about your material possessions and assets: your home, your car, your investments, your job. For others, it's having a partner or children that is of most significance.

Both examples are about ownership, and it's what this means to you personally that matters. There is a danger inherent in your sign of you slipping into wanting to possess status symbols or 'own' people for the wrong reasons.

This might be because you equate material objects with status and position and these are the reasons why you crave a bigger house, a more expensive car, another company to your name, etc.

In so doing, however, you have to be careful that you don't lose the pleasure in life or stop appreciating what you do have. Otherwise, you can carry on acquiring stuff for the sake of it, which can become ever more meaningless and superficial. Plus, you end up needing more and more in your life to satisfy your craving.

There is another level here that takes your Taurus archetype to the extreme, and this is to do with power and control. You start to feel powerful because of what you have, and you can become so fixated on your need for control or ownership that it reaches epic levels.

This becomes scary when your fixation is people or riches or territory, and power turns to domination. Absolute power can be misused and abused when it's held on to rigidly.

As a Taurus, one of your lessons is to learn about personal power. However, do so in a way that gives you inner strength and don't let a leaning towards power or ownership get out of hand.

This is where you can learn a lot from your opposite sign of Scorpio. Opposite signs of the zodiac take on each other's characteristics and learn from one another; whereas Taurus is linked to material matters and physical reality, Scorpio represents the metaphysical realm.

A true Scorpio knows it's not what you own in life that's important but what you learn about life. It's the deeper knowledge you gain, even if you have nothing, that can be invaluable. Scorpio understands too that power is a means to an end, and they use power to transform lives and bring about change for the better. Scorpio wields power then lets it go, rather than holding on fiercely in a fixed, dogged manner.

If you find yourself falling into the trap of believing that someone belongs to you or that you have a stubborn right to ownership regardless of the situation, take a step back. Loosen your grip and relax your stance.

When it comes to material possessions, remember it's only stuff at the end of the day, and it can be liberating for you as a Taurus to let it go. Also, there's a universal law that states when you hold on to the old, you prevent anything new coming into your life.

The same law applies to relationships; people are free agents to do as they choose. Notice where the Taurus resistance to change in your life works for you and where it works against you.

Your Star Sign Secrets

Shhh, don't tell anyone but your greatest fear is that other people will find out that you're jealous. From the outside, you like to look as if everything's fine, and it's true that your calm demeanour doesn't usually hide a whirlpool of painful emotions. And yet, you can get insanely jealous of other people's achievements/looks/perfect life – but you don't want anyone to know. This is Taurus' star sign secret.

You have another secret too. Even though you like to come across as eminently sensible and someone who has both feet firmly planted on the ground, you have a real fascination with all that is new-age. Trusting in life to guide you rather than taking practical steps to get where you want to be might seem daft to some, but it makes sense to you. You're not always that comfortable, however, declaring your new age beliefs or views.

Your Love Life

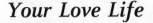

Knowing about your star sign is an absolute essential when it comes to love and relationships. Once you understand what drives you, nurtures you and keeps you happy in love, then you can be true to who you are rather than try to be someone you're not.

Plus, once you recognise your weak points when it comes to relationships (and everyone has them), you can learn to moderate them and focus instead on boosting your strengths to find happiness in love.

> **KEY CONCEPTS:** a committed relation-ship, a happy routine, emotional and financial security, sensual pleasures, finding a love that will last

Cosmic Tip: don't choose between love or money in a relationship, demand both.

Love and relationships are important for your sign of Taurus for different reasons. Firstly, finding a partner means you have someone with whom you can indulge your sensual nature. Affection and lovemaking can be a fulfilling part of your life, and a good sex life is often as important to you as food on the table and a roof over your head.

Lovemaking is free – theoretically – and sex on tap can make for a thrilled Taurus. More pleasure and enjoyment in life? Yes, please.

Secondly, being with a partner in life fulfils another Taurus need: the longing for security, for feeling safe, for being nurtured and looked after. If these are essential needs for you, then hooking up with a partner brings a new level of comfort and satisfaction to your life.

However, before leaping ahead it's important to note that for a typical Taurus, finding a partner isn't straightforward. Or at least, it can be challenging if you realise you're the one who has to make most of the running. Staying at home on the sofa watching TV every night isn't going to bring Mr/Ms Right any closer.

So be aware that the lazy side of your nature can hinder you if you're on the search for a loving relationship. And if you're genuinely seeking love or matrimony, then you need to play your part.

If you're a typical Taurus you won't be seeking a brief encounter either, although that's not to say you aren't capable of outrageous flirting if you so choose. You often meet a new partner when you're out with friends having a good time. A few drinks and some laughs help to unlock your inhibitions, and if Mr/Ms Body Beautiful comes your way, that will do nicely.

You have a great appreciation of the physical form, so looks matter to you, although ideally you want a partner with whom you're compatible. Top qualities for a Taurus partner are someone who's down to earth and has a good sense of humour, just like you. Money and security are also important, but that comes further down the line.

Another good idea if you're looking for love is to ask friends for an introduction. If they know you well, they're likely to come up with a good match, and it saves you having to put in a lot of work on the dating front.

Once you're in a relationship, you are one of the most loyal signs of the zodiac. Commitment and security are top values for you when it comes to love, and you can be a loving, caring and funny partner to the right person.

You often settle quickly into a new life as one half of a couple, and you enjoy being in a partnership that adds something extra to your own life. Meeting your partner's friends and family, seeing your other half most evenings and being invited to social events together at the weekend can make you very happy. This adds a level of comfort and routine to your life that suits your Taurus nature.

Money will be an important factor in any relationship, and ideally you want to be with someone who's financially independent, preferably loaded. Not necessarily, but if you're the type of Taurus who idealises a luxury lifestyle, then ensure that your partner's wealth matches your expectations.

At the very least, you're wise to be with someone who's solvent and who has similar values to your own. For you, partnership is often about building a life together and if you want your own family and a house in the country filled with kids and pets, then ensure you're in agreement.

If that's not your dream and you're more interested in pursuing other interests, e.g. buying properties or leading a worldwide laptop lifestyle, then again check up front that you want the same things as your partner. Being a money-conscious Taurus, you might even decide that taking out a prenuptial agreement is important to you.

It is essential that you don't rely entirely on appearances when it comes to love, but instead delve a little deeper. If you're true to your sign, you're an uncomplicated character, and quite often you keep your emotions hidden.

That doesn't apply to everyone, however, so get to know someone well before you make a commitment, and certainly find out whether any potential lover is keeping quiet about hidden secrets.

Once you're in a fulfilling relationship, there is very little that will shoehorn you out of it. As far as you're concerned, love is for keeps when you meet the person who makes you happy and promises you emotional and financial security.

It's rare for a Taurus to indulge in extramarital affairs unless there's something wrong with the relationship, because you seldom choose to rock the boat of love. Don't become too complacent, however, or allow your relationship or love life to become so routine and mundane that your partner grows bored. If every night ends with a quick back rub, two cups of cocoa and a good night's sleep, it's important that works for both of you.

You will fight tooth and nail for a relationship that matters to you, and you have the patience to wait out any competition or for love to improve if you're going through a rough patch. More than anything, however, you don't like to start over, which is why you won't give up easily on love or take kindly to your other half walking away.

Ultimately, you're looking for a committed relationship in life, and if you want to be together
until the end, as a tenacious Taurus you will do
your bit.

Your Love Matches

Some star signs are a better love match for you than others. The classic combinations are the other two star signs from the same element as your sign, earth; in Taurus' case, Virgo and Capricorn.

Sometimes the other earth signs can be too conventional or traditional for you, however, and you might be looking for a sparkier relationship, one in which opposites attract.

It's also important to recognise that any star sign match can be a good match if you're willing to learn from each other and use astrological insight to find out more about what makes the other person tick. Here's a quick guide to your love matches with all twelve star signs:

Taurus–Aries: Next-Door Neighbours

This is a sexy combination of the first two signs of the zodiac. Your sign is sensual and persistent, Aries is impulsive and bold. Aries teaches you that taking risks is a blast and you rein in head-strong Aries. Together you can have a lot of fun and achieve great things.

Taurus–Taurus: Two Peas In A Pod

A double dose of Taurus makes a delightful pairing as you both enjoy lovemaking and all forms of indulgence. A shared earthy sense of humour produces raucous laughter and naughty antics. You can build a dynamic business partnership and will love having lots of money to splash the cash.

Taurus–Gemini: Next-Door Neighbours

Your sign of Taurus loves comfort and routine, while Gemini is flighty and restless. You can enjoy a giggle together, but you both have to be prepared to meet the other halfway. You teach Gemini that consistency brings reward and Gemini's wit keeps you entertained.

Taurus–Cancer: Sexy Sextiles

Earth and water are in flow, and you and Cancer share a mutual love of food and comfort. It's an 'earth mother' combination, and healthy outdoor pursuits or a country lifestyle are all you two need to live happily ever after. Another ideal scenario is a big family to care for together.

Taurus–Leo: Squaring Up To Each Other

You two warm each other up and when you rub together the right way you create a passionate love. You both appreciate the good things in life and are happiest when you feel comfortable and are, preferably, well off. You can slip quickly into a routine, but Leo values constancy.

Taurus–Virgo: In Your Element

Routine and security are important issues for you both, and there's a mutual appreciation of what money can buy. You share a love of treats, healthy ones for Virgo particularly. A sensual match, both signs are body-oriented, and affection and touching go a long way to keeping the pleasure alive.

Taurus–Libra: Soulmates

Your sign of Taurus and Libra are the two signs of the zodiac ruled by romantic Venus. This is a warm and tender combination. You both have an innate understanding of the importance of beauty in the world and your immediate surroundings.

Taurus–Scorpio: Opposites Attract

Your sign rules money and the physical world, whereas Scorpio is the sign associated with life's hidden riches, intrigued by the metaphysical realm. Scorpio brings depth and intensity to your relationship, and you ground Scorpio in the real world. A passionate pairing.

Taurus–Sagittarius: Soulmates

Taurus and Sagittarius is an unlikely pairing at first glance: Taurus appreciates home comforts, and Sagittarius is the explorer of the zodiac. However, both signs are hedonists at heart and share a love of laughter and fun.

Taurus–Capricorn: In Your Element

You two can be great mates as well as lovers. You

like the good things in life and share a love of designer clothes and status symbols. Fresh air, good food and a sense of security create the sound basis from which this relationship can flourish and grow.

Taurus–Aquarius: Squaring Up To Each Other

Aquarius loves to be organised and will ensure that your creature comforts are catered for and then some. Aquarius can also be quirky and a breath of fresh air to your routine-loving ways. It's through your differences that you both learn to appreciate and understand the world better.

Taurus–Pisces: Sexy Sextiles

A romantic and deeply sensual partnership, this combination brings out the best in you both. The key to this relationship is whether you can ebb and flow together like the gentle lapping of the waves on a beach. Then you allow each other's creative and artistic nature to flourish and grow.

43

Your Sex Life

. . . . .

Being a Taurus, sensuality is your middle name, and if you're true to your Taurus nature, you'll be a hands-on lover. You're hugely affectionate, and if you don't have touch in your life, you can quickly become unhappy. You're a tactile person, and you need more than your fair share of hugs.

Lovemaking too is essential for you, especially in a close relationship. This is because it not only indulges your sensual nature but helps you feel secure and safe. Lying in your lover's arms can be incredibly comforting for the soft and gentle side of your Taurus nature.

There's a part of the Taurus temperament that's wholesome, which any amount of sexual experience cannot quench. You make a lover feel like they're the first and only lover in your life and that's a unique quality to have.

With your innate understanding of the human body and your love of pleasure, a classic Taurus is rarely shy when it comes to sex and lovemaking. Often for you, a regular sex life is an integral part of your relationship. Be careful that you don't fall into the Taurus trap of being too tired for sex or feel you can't be bothered.

You can be an expert in the lovemaking department, but you're potentially lazy and sometimes passive. Then you slip into the same routine in the bedroom and take the easy option. If you realise that you've chosen the missionary position for the umpteenth time, it might be a good idea to ring the changes, so you and your lover don't grow bored of each other.

That would be a shame because there are plenty of options to titillate the Taurus lover. You could choose to make love outdoors and go for alfresco sex in the countryside, for example.

Or perhaps experiment with your love of food and bring delectable delights into the bedroom. You're an aficionado of sensual indulgence, whether your delicacy of choice is chocolate, champagne or ice cream. Use all five senses to enhance your lovemaking and bring it to its fullest erotic potential.

If you're a typical Taurus, you'll be comfortable exploring your lover's body and allowing them to explore yours fully. You know instinctively that the human body is to be appreciated and that means taking your time and making love slowly. Touch, taste, smell, sight, hearing – focus on each sense individually and leave none out.

For a typical Taurus, there's no rush in the bedroom, and a slow pace can intensify the sensations of lovemaking. Cancel all appointments, turn off your phones and savour each stage of making love.

Your Taurus erogenous zone is the area around the throat, and you often love having your neck kissed while you're making love. Stroking and caressing each other creates maximum enjoyment and there's no race to the finish. Once you know what you want and like when it comes to physical pleasure, the sensual Taurus will instinctively keep the joys of lovemaking alive.

TAURUS ON A FIRST DATE

- you choose a restaurant that serves good food and plays great music

- you savour the whole experience slowly

- you like your date to take the lead conversationally

- you expect jokes and laughter – or no second date

- you have one too many drinks

Your Friends and Family

Friends play an important part in the life of a Taurus because you want people in your life to share the fun times with, whatever your pursuit of pleasure may be. Sitting at home on your own night after night becomes tedious, even for a relatively introspective sign of the zodiac like yourself.

Being around like-minded people brings out the best in you, and if sometimes you forget to live life to the full, always remember that your friends are there for you. They line up fun times, encourage you and get you out of the house when it's needed. Keep them around you at all times.

Friends are there for fun and laughter, for insight and gossip and for planning with, whether you want to go on holiday together or you inspire one another to play big in life. As a Taurus, you are excellent at sticking to a plan or goal once it's decided and getting excited about it, but you're not always brilliant at being spontaneous and having the motivation or spark in the first place.

As a friend yourself, you are incredibly loyal, you encourage others to see the funny side of life and you can be an absolute hoot to be around. Besides, you're a lifelong learner, and whatever you turn your hand to, you'll be thorough and a fount of knowledge. This is what friends often love about you: that you have tons of experience and insight to share and you will do so generously.

You can also laugh at yourself, and that's rarer than you think. Plus, you're an uncomplicated friend on the whole, because you call a spade a spade. If you're a typical Taurus, you're the opposite of a drama queen or king. In fact, it takes a lot for you to be provoked or lose your temper or throw a hissy fit. Although it's not out of the question, there must be a convincing reason to do so.

In general, you're accepting of others, although there is a side of your Taurus nature that friends and colleagues can find annoying. If someone's wrong, you have to point it out because a fact's a fact. Then if you refuse to back down, your stubborn nature kicks in, and that's when fall-outs can occur.

You are a kind friend, however, and you rarely hold on to grudges. There is one specific Taurus bugbear, and that's when friends borrow your stuff but don't give it back! In general, you're not trying to prove anything to other people, and you're happy for them to take you as you are and vice versa.

If anything, it's your fierce loyalty and your resistance to change that mean you sometimes put up with bad behaviour from friends way beyond what's really okay. You have to be pushed quite far before you turn your back and walk away, by which time your feelings may have been severely hurt.

In general, good friendships, like most of Taurus' close relationships, are for keeps. If you're typical of your sign, you'll have old friends from schooldays and will always make an effort to turn up for their special occasions. You're rarely a social butterfly but instead choose to have a few friends in your life who you cherish dearly.

Your generous Taurus nature means you will go to the ends of the earth and back for the ones you love, and you're a people person at heart. You care about family deeply, and you respect the bonds that tie you together.

You tend to enjoy the traditions of life, and regular family events often mean a lot to you. In fact, if you're a classic Taurus, you won't get bored with catching up with the same people year in, year out at the same venue. In their turn, family know what to expect from you and this consistency of character can be reassuring. You're genuine and sincere with the ones you love.

Children often play a significant role in your life because you like to nurture others. You might choose to have your own brood or be a proud godparent, auntie or uncle. You're a good choice for a guardian because you take your responsibilities seriously.

You respond to children on their level, and you like their matter-of-fact manner, especially while they're untarnished by the complexities of life.

54

You often adore children's sense of humour and their willingness to find the joy in life, however dirty, silly or crazy. There's a side of your Taurus nature that remains a big kid at heart, whatever your age.

Your Health and Well-Being

> **KEY CONCEPTS:** move your body, a love of food, pleasure and fitness, growing food and cooking it, at one with nature

The Taurus approach to health and well-being is always closely related to whether a sport/diet/ lifestyle makes you happy and gives you pleasure. This is often your default criterion when it comes to life in general.

Enjoyment is a fundamental element for you, and when you like what you do, and there's enough time in the day for leisure and indulgence, you tend to be a happy Taurus. And a happy Taurus is more likely to be a healthy Taurus.

Certainly feeling good about yourself and your life has a significant impact on your well-being. If life's all work and no play, if stress is a major component of every day, if people you're with make you sad rather than happy, your health will suffer.

If this is the case, the first symptom of illness you might notice as a Taurus is a sore throat, and this is usually a sign that your lifestyle is out of balance and your health needs a boost. Ensuring you get the right quantity of vitamins and minerals, through your diet and maybe supplements, is one way of taking care of yourself.

However, it is equally important for you to find your own form of keeping fit and active. If you slip into a sedentary lifestyle, with your Taurus predilection for food, you can quickly begin to feel unfit and tired.

Build regular exercise into your routine and at the very least ensure you get out in the fresh air every day and go for a walk. Playing golf is an excellent activity for your sign and being in nature arouses your senses.

You can take this one step further and get down and dirty with nature. Earth is your element, so sign up for a mud run or extreme assault course. Mud is good for you as a Taurus, whether you choose to bathe in it or wear it as a face pack.

Motivation can be a struggle for you on your own, and if so it works to buddy up with someone close and go to the gym together or hire a personal trainer. You have a natural rhythm, so get your body moving and sign up for dance or movement classes or hit the dance floor on a night out with friends.

Enjoying whatever you do physically means you're likely to do more of it. This is a better strategy for you than trying to attain discipline in your life for the sake of it.

Don't forget one of the best forms of physical exercise either – lovemaking – as this taps into the sensual side of your nature and has the added bonus of increasing your heart rate.

You are a sign of the zodiac who loves the human body and having a massage on a regular basis would be wonderful for you. This can be one of your best forms of relaxation. Stretching too is good for you, so consider a yoga or Pilates class.

You might also choose to go nude. If you're fully in tune with your body-loving Taurus nature, then let it all hang out. You could head for a naturist beach, join in with a naked bike ride or, if that's a step too far, start by walking barefoot in nature. This can be a great way of rekindling your love and appreciation of the human body and of nature at the same time. Being a Taurus, you're an earth child and blessed with Venusian sensuality. Love your body, love nature, love your life.

Taurus and Food

If you're a typical Taurus, you will love your food, both eating it and cooking it. In fact, you are one of two signs of the zodiac, the other being Cancer, who is most likely to enjoy working in the world of food.

You have a healthy appetite and can appreciate home cooking, regional cooking on your travels and the high end of the market, the fine dining experience. If someone wants to find the way to your heart, they could start by cooking a delicious meal for you.

You teach others how to savour food, and a typical Taurus enjoys nothing more than a long luxurious meal, preferably outside, with friends and family. It's sacrilege in your eyes to rush the partaking of food.

Being a Taurus, you're not usually someone who veers towards faddy diets or will put up with a fast food lifestyle. You prefer quality food items in line with your pleasurable approach to life. Having an empty fridge isn't good for the Taurus soul.

However, your love of food does mean that you can put on weight easily. In this case, you would be happier on a high-fat diet and cutting back on carbohydrates rather than put up with an extreme calorie-counting regime, which can be your idea of food hell.

Many fruits are ruled by Venus, your planet, so starting the day with a glass of healthy juice often works for you – apples, pears or berries. Or if you're not feeling the need to be super-healthy, you could turn them into a crumble with lashings of cream or custard. Artichoke and asparagus are Taurus foods too, as are wheat, cloves and mixed spices.

You might be the type of Taurus who likes to grow your own food. A vegetable patch or allotment not only ensures your food is organic, but also gives you the chance to be outside and tending to plants. Nurturing is an essential characteristic of your Taurus nature; this is where the 'earth mother' side of your personality comes to the fore.

You can nurture and grow your food, take it inside and nourish and cook for the ones you love. Whether you're making jams and pickles to give as presents or you're baking cakes and cookies for a special occasion, this is where the archetypal Taurus comes into their own.

Do You Look Like A Taurus?

You are one of two signs of the zodiac to be blessed with the goddess of beauty, Venus, as your ruling planet, the other one being Libra. You tend to have a natural earthy beauty, and your movement is often slow and sensual.

The classic Taurus face is gorgeous to look at, whether male or female. The female Taurus often has rosebud lips and big 'cow' eyes, and the male is no less beautiful. Your face shape is usually round or square with a broad forehead, heavy eyebrows and a well-defined jawline.

Taurus rules the throat and neck, and this can be a distinguishing feature for you, whether you have a stocky bull-like neck or a graceful swanlike one. Your voice is often melodious, and you're one of the zodiac's most talented singers. Other people often notice you first by your voice.

Your Style and Image

It's rare to find a slender Taurus because your ruler Venus is all about sensuality and indulgence. Your sign is more in tune with curvaceous lines and a voluptuous figure in the women and a stocky, muscular physique in the men. Thus, you suit clothes that are comfortable, soft fabrics and figure-hugging materials.

Thanks to Venus, a typical Taurus has expensive tastes, and you're likely to choose quality items of clothing over cheaper versions. That doesn't mean you won't have an eye for a bargain or the patience to wait for the sales, but generally, you invest in outfits that fit your lifestyle. Tailored garments and classic-cut suits can look fantastic on you.

Natural materials, such as suede, leather and denim, are often an intrinsic part of the Taurus wardrobe – the cowgirl or cowboy look. Unless, of course, you're the dippy hippy type of Taurus who prefers to buy vegan or non-leather shoes, belts and bags.

Your style veers towards the feminine, whether male or female. The Taurus man is often the epitome of masculinity, robust and powerful, but with a love of grooming and strong aftershave. David Beckham (2 May) even pulled off wearing a sarong back in the day.

The Taurus woman can effortlessly team a silk blouse with a pair of jeans or will be attracted to items of clothing that have bows, a flower design or are made from faux fur. Softness and sensation go hand in hand.

Pink is one of your favourite colours, and Taurus men look great in a pink shirt. V-neck or low-cut tops are a must to show off your neck or cleavage. The best jewellery you can wear is a necklace or chain that highlights your Taurus beauty spot, the throat. Green or emerald jewellery is a stunning choice and fits your Venusian style.

You might be the type of Taurus who veers towards the luxury lifestyle and wants to invest in opulent clothes and accessories that will last a lifetime. Or perhaps you're more geared up for comfort and clothes that you can move in easily and which suit your down-to-earth, natural style. Either way, your sign often gains a lot of enjoyment from what you wear and how it makes you feel.

Your Home

Your Ideal Taurus Home:

Think of a beautiful countryside on a summer day with its warm tones and rich hues, and that's Taurus' style. Your dream home would be a country cottage where you can be close to nature.

When it comes to the home, yours is the star sign that values security the most. If you don't have a place you can call home, it can be hard for you to function well.

For you, as a Taurus, comfort and stability are paramount – your element is earth, and your natural qualities are steadiness and dependability. Other people view you as the 'earth mother' type, someone who enjoys the simple pleasures in life, like cooking, eating, hugging and relating.

Usually, you prefer a home to be lived-in rather than a show home. Ideally, one room in your home will be a haven and burrow of domesticity. A kitchen with a big table where people can gather, eat and be nourished and feel safe and warm suits your Taurus nature. Or for you person- ally – a bathroom filled with candles and sweet-smelling bath oils, your own private space where you can relax.

In general, you tend to be a traditionalist when it comes to home styling, and you appreciate quality. Taurus style includes classic designs, and you lean towards gentle curves and draping soft fabrics, rather than straight-cut or rigid furniture.

As you are one of the earth signs, there should be plenty of natural materials around the place – you often love tweed, wool and cashmere or have a fluffy sheepskin rug centre stage. When it comes to furniture, choose wood – oak, ash and pine. You also like furniture that's low so you can be closer to the ground.

You expect any purchases to last, so things around the home must be robust and durable. You won't skimp and save, although that's not to say you don't have an eye for a bargain – you do, but you also have class.

An archetypal Taurus deplores anything ugly, stark or even too modern. The colours associated with your sign are greens, rust, copper and earthy browns, all the colours of nature. Pink too gets a look-in, thanks to your ruling planet Venus.

If you live in town, even a small garden will appeal, or at the very least a window box or pot plants so that you have colour and greenery around you. Or choose a picture of a pastoral scene and bring the countryside into your home.

Being a Taurus, you're not a lover of change. Although you would be happy renovating an old house to suit your tastes, once you've got your surroundings to your liking, you're more likely to stay put. Other people may think you're lazy, but you think of it more as being satisfied with your situation.

You could even have your own comfy chair that goes everywhere with you, somewhere you can snuggle up, stop and relax. Comfort is paramount in Taurus' world.

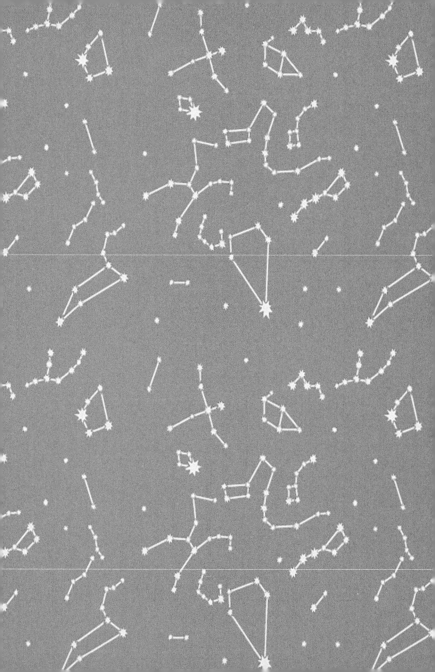

Your Star Sign Destinations

IDEAS FOR TAURUS:

- *a week in Ireland learning the Irish jig*

- *a beach holiday complete with hammock and cocktails*

- *a cookery course or painting holiday in Greece*

Did you know that many cities and countries are ruled by a particular star sign? This is based on when a country is founded, although sometimes, depending on their history, places have more than one star sign attributed to them.

This can help you decide where to go on holiday, and it can also be why there are certain places where you feel at home straight away.

Being a Taurus and one of the earth signs, you love the countryside, and anywhere with rolling green hills and an abundance of nature is ideal for a short or long break. Head for a health spa in Switzerland to immerse yourself fully in a sense-tastic Taurus experience.

If you live in the city, it's even more important that you get out of town once in a while and go somewhere that has space and soul-boosting views and where you can breathe in fresh air.

A typical Taurus prefers holidays closer to home, anywhere that's easy to get to and isn't too much of a faff travel-wise. Long-haul destinations can put you off, partly because of the jet lag; trains are usually preferable for a Taurus rather than planes. Plus, anywhere that's incredibly hot is rarely top of your holiday hit list.

Safety, however, is essential and one of your first questions is often whether your hotel has a private safe in the rooms.

You prefer holiday destinations where you can take in a spot of culture, enjoy good food and have a relaxing break. You benefit from the feel of the sun on your body as well as a gentle breeze. A romantic holiday that gives you plenty of time for sex and romance can also hit all the right spots.

You are a creature of habit if you're a typical Taurus. This means that if you find a place that's ideal for you, you're likely to go back time and again. Being ruled by lavish Venus, you're not averse to five-star luxury, but you could be just as happy with a home swap, or a home-from-home experience visiting good friends. Optimal relaxing and little stress is the Taurus way.

Countries ruled by Taurus include Ireland, Switzerland, Iran, Cyprus, the Greek Islands

Cities ruled by Taurus include Hastings in the UK; Dublin in Ireland; Würzburg and Leipzig in Germany; Parma and Capri in Italy; St Louis in the USA

Your Career and Vocation

> **KEY CONCEPTS:** a regular job, a hands-on profession, the natural world, money and art, comfort and security

Being a Taurus and one of the earth signs means you thrive on routine and safety is important to you in work as in life. In fact, you're often happiest in regular employment as you're not someone who thrives on a 'boom or bust' lifestyle. Not knowing where your next pay cheque is coming from can make you very edgy.

You tend to appreciate reliability and constancy in your routine. The fact that you can do the same job day in, day out and not have to worry too much about the details often appeals to you.

You're someone who usually finds it easy to get on with a job rather than needing outside stimulation or extra motivation. You work well on your own and even when you work alongside other people, you don't need a lot of supervision or additional support.

This is one of your core strengths: that you're dependable, and other people are happy leaving you to hold the fort, to be a reliable member of the team. At your best, your sign is 100% responsible and trustworthy.

However, that's not to say you're always going to be the sensible one at work. If you're happy with what you do, it shows in your personality and you, more than many other of the star signs, like to have a laugh and a joke. Working in an environment with a gloomy team of people would soon bring you down.

It's good for you to have a profession that keeps you busy. Your ruling planet Venus can sway you towards an indulgent lifestyle, and if you get into a lazy routine, sometimes it can be hard for you to break out of a period of lethargy.

Hands-on professions are made for your sign. Working in a trade that enables you to use your hands and earn you good money ticks a lot of Taurus boxes. You might be a builder, a construction worker or any other profession where you get to make things and be productive.

If you're a physically strong Taurus, you can take on any physical business and excel. Agriculture and farming are classic Taurus careers, and if you're true to your sign you don't mind getting your hands dirty and mucking in. You often love working outside.

Art is Taurus' domain, and you like to create things of beauty. Your sign is expert at working with natural materials to make something that's beautiful to behold. You might feel at home with plants and in the natural world, or use natural materials to make sculpture, art or furniture.

There's a graceful side to the Taurus character, which is unlike your zodiac symbol the Bull but more in tune with your feminine Venusian side. In fact, inside many a Taurus there's a dancer, singer or musician just waiting to get out.

Margot Fonteyn (18 May) and Darcey Bussell (27 April) channelled their Venus grace into ballet dancing and one of the most legendary dancers of all time, who had Taurus twinkle toes, was Fred Astaire (10 May).

As a Taurus, you tend to be at ease in your own

body, and you often have a real love of the physical form. Whether you collect nudes in art, fancy yourself as a life model or work in a medical profession, you can be a natural when it comes to all aspects of the human body.

You're rarely happy in a business where your work isn't valued and, being a practical Taurus, it's important that you feel useful or to work in an industry that brings about tangible results.

You can turn your hand to most forms of established business, and if you're a typical Taurus, you love dealing with money. Banking, accounting and financial planning are sound careers for you, and you're a wise choice to help people make money with money.

It is worth noting however that you're not usually comfortable with a high-risk strategy, in life or at work. In fact, your sign of Taurus tends to be risk-averse, so you might not be happy dealing with a financial situation that could lose you a lot of money overnight. That would be your worst nightmare.

Sometimes too, your resistance to change means that you get stuck in a job or profession for too long. You opt for security and comfort rather than advancement or a change of career. It's worth questioning now and again whether settling for a comfortable life is the right decision for you in the long term.

If you're seeking inspiration for a new job, take a look at the list below, which reveals the traditional careers that come under the Taurus archetype:

TRADITIONAL TAURUS CAREERS

builder
construction worker
banker
financial planner
ballet dancer
fashion model

artist

potter

furniture maker

gardener

botanist

naturalist

farmer

singer

musician

comedian

jewellery maker

art dealer

masseur

confectioner

Your Money and Prosperity

> **KEY CONCEPTS:** sound business sense, use money to make money, investing in property and products, low-risk strategy

If you're true to your sign of Taurus, you have a natural affinity with money. Your sign rules the second house in astrology, which governs money and possessions, values and resources.

You love buying and investing, and you often have a good eye for what's going to have lasting value. You can do well with real-estate and property deals, and you enjoy having something tangible for your money that you can see and touch.

In fact, you often like to own your home because it taps into the side of your nature that wants and needs to feel secure, both emotionally and financially. Renting can be too risky for you, although it could also be viewed as an exciting challenge, stepping out of your comfort zone.

If you're a typical Taurus, possessions are important to you, and you can accumulate a lot of stuff throughout your lifetime. You are the type of person who would hold on to an heirloom or precious object because it might increase in value over time.

You approach money and savings in the same way, and you tend to hold on to a nest egg in case of the proverbial 'rainy day'. This isn't, however, always the best strategy. If you trust more in the flow of money and consider your alternatives, you might make life easier and more enjoyable by taking a more adventurous approach to money and prosperity.

In particular, it's worth looking at any fears you have around money and noticing whether holding on too tight limits other options for you. Being a security-loving Taurus, however, even a shed you could call your own would probably be preferable to a more free-wheeling existence.

You are comfortable in the world of money because you go about things in a practical, efficient manner. You don't miss out on the facts and figures stage, and instead, you're often thorough and will ensure that no mistakes are made. You have a sound business head and good common sense, and these skills are invaluable when it comes to increasing your wealth.

Other people might accuse you of being tight with money, but usually it's just because you have a strong sense of self-preservation and you place high value on money and what's yours. If anything, you have a high regard for money, which is why you keep close tabs on it, and you're not careless or overly generous.

When it comes to your appreciation of money, the Taurus stereotype falls into two camps. You might be the type of Taurus who knows that you want to lead an opulent luxury lifestyle and will plan your life accordingly. If this is the case, you tend to work your way up the ladder diligently, making excellent business and money decisions along the way.

Alternatively, if you're more in tune with the hippy side of your Taurus character, you would be satisfied with a slow lifestyle that allows you plenty of time to relax in nature. Then you would decide to forgo riches in place of simple natural pleasures and be as happy camping as staying in five-star accommodation. Unless someone else is paying, of course!

How you view money, what it represents to you and where your real values lie are all important Taurus lessons to learn. Do what's right for you and happiness will follow.

Your Cosmic Gifts and Talents

Staying Power

Yours is the sign of endurance and longevity, and once you start something, you're in it for the long run. This can be a brilliant strength in many different areas of life, e.g. when you want to bed in a habit, prove yourself to be indispensable, get through a rough patch, be the anchor, the rock, the dependable one.

Queen Elizabeth II (21 April), who has reigned as monarch of the United Kingdom and the Commonwealth for over sixty-five years, is the typical Taurus. Staying power has also proved handy for the Taurus Brownlee brothers, Alistair (23 April) and Jonny (30 April), who've conquered the world of triathlon. If ever there was an endurance performer in athletics, it's got to be the triathlete.

Love The Earth

You have a natural affinity with the earth. Not only are you one of the three earth signs but your ruling planet is Venus. Venus revels in the sensual world and nature is one area of life that promises a heightening of all five senses – sight, smell, sound, touch and taste. Nature is where simple pleasures abound, where plants can be nurtured and contribute to the environment, where food can be grown and subsequently enjoyed.

It's a fertile environment that is essential to our continued life on earth. So consider how you can play a role in extolling the vital importance of nature's role in the world. David Attenborough (8 May), naturalist, wildlife and plant life expert, is an excellent example of how your sign of Taurus can honour the earth.

Healing Hugs

With your natural instinct for touch and physical connection, you are one of the zodiac's healers. Whether you love giving a massage, you're an advocate of the Free Hugs campaign or you choose to care for and nurture pets, children or adults, use your Taurus healing powers to good effect. The world needs more healing hugs, and you're one of the best huggers.

The Voice

Your voice can be your passport to fame and fortune and if you have a distinctive sound, use it. The Taurus tone might be smooth or gravelly, baritone or soprano; but if your voice stands out, set up a podcast, be a radio host, speak in public or tell stories.

As Taurus rules the throat, it's no surprise that there are a ton of brilliant singers born under your sign, Adele (5 May), Stevie Wonder (13 May), Kelly Clarkson (24 April) and Ella Fitzgerald (25 April) to name a few. If you're a typical Taurus, you've got rhythm; you love music, so harmonise, join a choir, sing your way through life.

Spread Laughter

You are one of the zodiac's comedians and one of your natural gifts is to fill the world with fun, jokes and laughter. One of the best known and most celebrated dramatists of all time is Taurus William Shakespeare and his work is full of comedy and bawdy humour. He may have penned his works 400 years ago, but his natural talent for jokes and japes continues to amuse audiences today. You might choose to be a stand-up comedian, a classic Taurus profession, but even if not, spread fun and laughter.

Be Stubborn

It might sound like an odd cosmic gift or talent to have, but being stubborn can be a tremendous strength and one you want to channel in all the right ways. Being stubborn means that you will not give up on a goal and you will go to remarkable levels to fulfil a promise or take a stand. If anyone can achieve the impossible and show incredible resilience and stamina in life, it's your sign of Taurus. Give up? Never!

The Tortoise Wins

If you're a Taurus and you don't yet know Aesop's famous fable 'The Tortoise And The Hare', then it's a must-read. It's a story of two unequal partners, one of whom represents the strength of the twin values of doggedness and persistence, excellent Taurus qualities.

Taurus hates to be rushed or to hurry; this is when mistakes are made. Instead, you know that when you take your time and continue steadily along the same path without distraction, you are more likely to reach your destination safely and successfully. This is Taurus' way: 'less haste, more speed.'

Films, Books, Music

• • • • •

Films: *It's a Wonderful Life,* director Frank Capra (18 May) and starring James Stewart (20 May) or *Citizen Kane,* starring, directed and produced by Orson Welles (6 May)

Books: Any works by William Shakespeare (23 April), *Jane Eyre* by Charlotte Brontë (21 April) or *To Kill A Mockingbird* by Harper Lee (28 April)

Music: A range of musical genres to please the Taurus ear: rock – U2, lead singer, Bono (10 May), soul music – James Brown (3 May), contemporary R&B – Sam Smith (19 May) or country – Willie Nelson (29 April)

YOGA POSE:

Bridge: strengthens neck and shoulders, keeps
the spine flexible

TAROT CARD:

The Empress

GIFTS TO BUY A TAURUS:

- colour therapy book and set of pens
- a pair of Birkenstocks
- massage voucher
- inflatable hammock
- a portable greenhouse
- vintage wine
- a sculpture for the garden or home
- cookbooks, organic or gourmet
- designer handbag or man purse
- Star Gift – a holistic or study holiday

Taurus Celebrities Born On Your Birthday

APRIL

 Joan Miró, Luther Vandross, Jessica Lange, Carmen Electra, Ryan O'Neal

 Queen Elizabeth II, Charlotte Brontë, Anthony Quinn, Iggy Pop, Nicholas Lyndhurst, Andie MacDowell, James McAvoy, Steve Backshall

22 Jack Nicholson, Charles Mingus, Glen Campbell, Jeffrey Dean Morgan, Amber Heard, Louis Smith, Issy Miyake

 23 William Shakespeare, Shirley Temple, William Roache, Michael Moore, John Cena, John Hannah, Dev Patel, Gigi Hadid, Alistair Brownlee, Roy Orbison

 24 Shirley MacLaine, Len Goodman, Barbra Streisand, Jean-Paul Gaultier, Paula Yates, Gabby Logan, Kelly Clarkson, Tyson Ritter, Caspar Lee

 25 Ella Fitzgerald, Al Pacino, Renée Zellweger

26 Jet Li, Melania Trump, Channing Tatum

27 Sheena Easton, Darcey Bussell, Tess Daly, Jenna Coleman

Jay Leno, Ann-Margret, Jorge Garcia, Vernon Kay, Penélope Cruz, Jessica Alba, Izzy Bizu

 Duke Ellington, Anita Dobson, Jerry Seinfeld, Daniel Day-Lewis, Michelle Pfeiffer, Paul Adelstein, Andre Agassi, Uma Thurman, Kian Egan

 Willie Nelson, Leslie Grantham, Jane Campion, Adrian Pasdar, Kirsten Dunst, Ashley Dupre, Jonny Brownlee, Leigh Francis, Sam Heughan, Travis Scott

MAY

 Wes Anderson, Joseph Heller, Una Stubbs, Joanna Lumley, Tim McGraw, Matt Di Angelo, Jamie Dornan, Wes Welker, John Woo

2 Bianca Jagger, David Suchet, Alan Titchmarsh, Dwayne Johnson, David Beckham, Lily Allen, Princess Charlotte

3 Bing Crosby, James Brown, Ken Hom, Kirsty Wark, Jo Brand, Ben Elton, Rob Brydon, Sandi Toksvig, Christina Hendricks, Suzi Perry

4 Audrey Hepburn, Michael Barrymore, Randy Travis, Lance Bass, Rory McIlroy

5 Rudolph Valentino, Tammy Wynette, Michael Palin, Richard E. Grant, Richard Blackwood, Chris Brown, Henry Cavill, Adele

6 Orson Welles, Tony Blair, George Clooney, Gabourey Sidibe

7 Eva Perón

David Attenborough, Enrique Iglesias, Martha Wainwright, Matt Willis

 Howard Carter, Candice Bergen, Glenda Jackson, Billy Joel, Matthew Kelly, Rosario Dawson

 Fred Astaire, Maureen Lipman, Wayne Dyer, Bono, Linda Evangelista, Sid Vicious

 Irving Berlin, Salvador Dalí, Jeremy Paxman, David Gest, Natasha Richardson, Cam Newton, Blac Chyna, Cory Monteith, Laetitia Casta

 Katharine Hepburn, Tony Hancock, Burt Bacharach, Emilio Estevez, Jason Biggs, Ian Dury

 Harvey Keitel, Judy Finnigan, Zoë Wanamaker, Stevie Wonder, Dennis Rodman, Richard Madeley, Samantha

Morton, Robert Pattinson, Lena
Dunham

 Eric Morecambe, George Lucas, Cate
Blanchett, Sofia Coppola, Natalie
Appleton, David Byrne, Mark Zuckerberg,
Olly Murs, Miranda Cosgrove

 Brian Eno, Greg Wise, Zara Phillips,
Jamie-Lynn Sigler, Andy Murray, Jasper
Johns, Nicola Walker

Henry Fonda, Liberace, Pierce
Brosnan, Debra Winger, Janet Jackson,
Tori Spelling, Megan Fox, Thomas
Brodie-Sangster

Dennis Hopper, Simon Fuller, Jeremy
Vine, Enya, Andrea Corr, Derek Hough

Margot Fonteyn, Frank Capra, Tina Fey,
George Strait, Jack Johnson, Sam Smith

Malcolm X, Nora Ephron, Pete Townsend, Grace Jones, Victoria Wood

 James Stewart, Cher, Louis Theroux, Busta Rhymes

Q&A Section

• • • • •

Q. What is the difference between a Sun sign and a Star sign?

A. They are the same thing. The Sun spends one month in each of the twelve star signs every year, so if you were born on 1 January, you are a Sun Capricorn. In astronomy, the Sun is termed a star rather than a planet, which is why the two names are interchangeable. The term 'zodiac sign', too, means the same as Sun sign and Star sign and is another way of describing which one of the twelve star signs you are, e.g. Sun Capricorn.

Q. What does it mean if I'm born on the cusp?

A. Being born on the cusp means that you were born on a day when the Sun moves from one of the twelve zodiac signs into the next. However, the Sun doesn't change signs at the same time each year. Sometimes it can be a day earlier or a day later. In the celebrity birthday section of the book, names in brackets mean that this person's birthday falls into this category.

If you know your complete birth data, including the date, time and place you were born, you can find out definitively what Sun sign you are. You do this by either checking an ephemeris (a planetary table) or asking an astrologer. For example, if a baby were born on 20 January 2018, it would be Sun Capricorn if born before 03:09 GMT or Sun Aquarius if born after 03:09 GMT. A year earlier, the Sun left Capricorn a day earlier and entered Aquarius on 19 January 2017, at 21:24 GMT. Each year the time changes are slightly different.

Q. Has my sign of the zodiac changed since I was born?

A. Every now and again, the media talks about a new sign of the zodiac called Ophiuchus and about there now being thirteen signs. This means that you're unlikely to be the same Sun sign as you always thought you were.

This method is based on fixing the Sun's movement to the star constellations in the sky, and is called 'sidereal' astrology. It's used traditionally in India and other Asian countries.

The star constellations are merely namesakes for the twelve zodiac signs. In western astrology, the zodiac is divided into twelve equal parts that are in sync with the seasons. This method is called 'tropical' astrology. The star constellations and the zodiac signs aren't the same.

Astrology is based on a beautiful pattern of symmetry (see Additional Information) and it wouldn't be the same if a thirteenth sign were introduced into the pattern. So never fear, no one is going to have to say their star sign is Ophiuchus, a name nobody even knows how to pronounce!

Q. Is astrology still relevant to me if I was born in the southern hemisphere?

A. Yes, astrology is unquestionably relevant to you. Astrology's origins, however, were founded in the northern hemisphere, which is why the Spring Equinox coincides with the Sun's move into Aries, the first sign of the zodiac. In the southern hemisphere, the seasons are reversed. Babylonian, Egyptian and Greek and Roman astrology are the forebears of modern-day astrology, and all of these civilisations were located in the northern hemisphere.

* * * * *

Q. Should I read my Sun sign, Moon sign and Ascendant sign?

A. If you know your horoscope or you have drawn up an astrology wheel for the time of your birth, you will be aware that you are more than your Sun sign. The Sun is the most important star in the sky, however, because the other planets revolve around it, and your horoscope in the media is based on Sun signs. The Sun represents your essence, who you are striving to become throughout your lifetime.

The Sun, Moon and Ascendant together give
you a broader impression of yourself as all three
reveal further elements about your personality.
If you know your Moon and Ascendant signs,
you can read all three books to gain further
insight into who you are. It's also a good idea to
read the Sun sign book that relates to your
partner, parents, children, best friends, even
your boss for a better understanding of their
characters too.

Q. Is astrology a mix of fate and free will?

A. Yes. Astrology is not causal, i.e. the planets
don't cause things to happen in your life;
instead, the two are interconnected, hence the
saying 'As above, so below'. The symbolism
of the planets' movements mirrors what's
happening on earth and in your personal
experience of life.

You can choose to sit back and let your life
unfold, or you can decide the best course of

action available to you. In this way, you are combining your fate and free will, and this is one of astrology's major purposes in life. A knowledge of astrology can help you live more authentically, and it offers you a fresh perspective on how best to make progress in your life.

Q. What does it mean if I don't identify with my Sun sign? Is there a reason for this?

A. The majority of people identify with their Sun sign, and it is thought that one route to fulfilment is to grow into your Sun sign. You do get the odd exception, however.

For example, a Pisces man was adamant that he wasn't at all romantic, mystical, creative or caring, all typical Pisces archetypes. It turned out he'd spent the whole of his adult life working in the oil industry and lived primarily on the sea. Neptune is one of Pisces' ruling planets and god of the sea and Pisces rules all liquids, including oil. There's the Pisces connection.

Q. What's the difference between astrology and astronomy?

A. Astrology means 'language of the stars', whereas astronomy means 'mapping of the stars'. Traditionally, they were considered one discipline, one form of study and they coexisted together for many hundreds of years. Since the dawn of the Scientific Age, however, they have split apart.

Astronomy is the scientific strand, calculating and logging the movement of the planets, whereas astrology is the interpretation of the movement of the stars. Astrology works on a symbolic and intuitive level to offer guidance and insight. It reunites you with a universal truth, a knowingness that can sometimes get lost in place of an objective, scientific truth. Both are of value.

Q. What is a cosmic marriage in astrology?

A. One of the classic indicators of a relationship that's a match made in heaven is the union of the Sun and Moon. When they fall close to each other in the same sign in the birth charts of you and your partner, this is called a cosmic marriage. In astrology, the Sun and Moon are the king and queen of the heavens; the Sun is a masculine energy, and the Moon a feminine energy. They represent the eternal cycle of day and night, yin and yang.

Q. What does the Saturn Return mean?

A. In traditional astrology, Saturn was the furthest planet from the Sun, representing boundaries and the end of the universe. Saturn is linked to karma and time, and represents authority, structure and responsibility. It takes Saturn twenty-nine to thirty years to make a complete cycle of the zodiac and return to the place where it was when you were born.

This is what people mean when they talk about their Saturn Return; it's the astrological coming of age. Turning thirty can be a soul-searching time, when you examine how far you've come in life and whether you're on the right track. It's a watershed moment, a reality check and a defining stage of adulthood. The decisions you make during your Saturn Return are crucial, whether they represent endings or new commitments. Either way, it's the start of an important stage in your life path.

Additional Information

· · · · ·

The Symmetry of Astrology

There is a beautiful symmetry to the zodiac (see horoscope wheel). There are twelve zodiac signs, which can be divided into two sets of 'introvert' and 'extrovert' signs, four elements (fire, earth, air, water), three modes (cardinal, fixed, mutable) and six pairs of opposite signs.

One of the values of astrology is in bringing opposites together, showing how they complement each other and work together and, in so doing, restore unity. The horoscope wheel represents the cyclical nature of life.

Aries (*March 21–April 19*)
Taurus (*April 20–May 20*)
Gemini (*May 21–June 20*)
Cancer (*June 21–July 22*)
Leo (*July 23–August 22*)
Virgo (*August 23–September 22*)
Libra (*September 23–October 23*)
Scorpio (*October 24–November 22*)
Sagittarius (*November 23–December 21*)
Capricorn (*December 22–January 20*)
Aquarius (*January 21–February 18*)
Pisces (*February 19–March 20*)

ELEMENTS

There are four elements in astrology and three signs allocated to each. The elements are:

fire – Aries, Leo, Sagittarius
earth – Taurus, Virgo, Capricorn
air – Gemini, Libra, Aquarius
water – Cancer, Scorpio, Pisces

What each element represents:

Fire – fire blazes bright and fire types are inspirational, motivational, adventurous and love creativity and play

Earth – earth is grounding and solid, and earth rules money, security, practicality, the physical body and slow living

Air – air is intangible and vast and air rules thinking, ideas, social interaction, debate and questioning

Water – water is deep and healing and water rules feelings, intuition, quietness, relating, giving and sharing

MODES

There are three modes in astrology and four star signs allocated to each. The modes are:

cardinal – Aries, Cancer, Libra, Capricorn
fixed – Taurus, Leo, Scorpio, Aquarius
mutable – Gemini, Virgo, Sagittarius, Pisces

What each mode represents:

Cardinal – The first group represents the leaders of the zodiac, and these signs love to initiate and take action. Some say they're controlling.

Fixed – The middle group holds fast and stands the middle ground and acts as a stable, reliable companion. Some say they're stubborn.

Mutable – The last group is more willing to go with the flow and let life drift. They're more flexible and adaptable and often dual-natured. Some say they're all over the place.

INTROVERT AND EXTROVERT SIGNS/ OPPOSITE SIGNS

The introvert signs are the earth and water signs and the extrovert signs are the fire and air signs. Both sets oppose each other across the zodiac.

The 'introvert' earth and water oppositions are:

- Taurus – • Scorpio
- Cancer – • Capricorn
- Virgo – • Pisces

The 'extrovert' air and fire oppositions are:

- Aries – • Libra
- Gemini – • Sagittarius
- Leo – • Aquarius

THE HOUSES

The houses of the astrology wheel are an additional component to Sun sign horoscopes. The symmetry that is inherent within astrology remains, as the wheel is divided into twelve equal sections, called 'houses'. Each of the twelve houses is governed by one of the twelve zodiac signs.

There is an overlap in meaning as you move round the houses. Once you know the symbolism of all the star signs, it can be fleshed out further by learning about the areas of life represented by the twelve houses.

The houses provide more specific information if you choose to have a detailed birth chart reading.

This is based not only on your day of birth, which reveals your star sign, but also your time and place of birth. Here's the complete list of the meanings of the twelve houses and the zodiac sign they are ruled by:

1 – **Aries:** self, physical body, personal goals

2 – **Taurus:** money, possessions, values

3 – **Gemini:** communication, education, siblings, local neighbourhood

4 – **Cancer:** home, family, roots, the past, ancestry

5 – **Leo:** creativity, romance, entertainment, children, luck

6 – **Virgo:** work, routine, health, service

7 – **Libra:** relationships, the 'other', enemies, contracts

8 – **Scorpio:** joint finances, other peoples' resources, all things hidden and taboo

9 – **Sagittarius:** travel, study, philosophy, legal affairs, publishing, religion

10 – **Capricorn:** career, vocation, status, reputation

11 – **Aquarius:** friends, groups, networks, social responsibilities

12 – **Pisces:** retreat, sacrifice, spirituality

A GUIDE TO LOVE MATCHES

The star signs relate to each other in different ways depending on their essential nature. It can also be helpful to know the pattern they create across the zodiac. Here's a quick guide that relates to the chapter on Love Matches:

Two Peas In A Pod – the same star sign

Opposites Attract – star signs opposite each other

Soulmates – five or seven signs apart, and a traditional 'soulmate' connection

In Your Element – four signs apart, which means you share the same element

Squaring Up To Each Other – three signs apart, which means you share the same mode

Sexy Sextiles – two signs apart, which means you're both 'introverts' or 'extroverts'

Next Door Neighbours – one sign apart, different in nature but often share close connections